A Robbie Reader

# What's So Great About . . . ?

# CHRISTOPHER COLUMBUS

Amie Jane Leavitt

P.O. Box 196
Hockessin, Delaware 19707
Visit us on the web: www.mitchelllane.com
Comments? email us: mitchelllane@mitchelllane.com

Printing     1        2        3        4        5        6        7        8        9

### A Robbie Reader/What's So Great About . . . ?

| | | |
|---|---|---|
| Amelia Earhart | Anne Frank | Annie Oakley |
| **Christopher Columbus** | Daniel Boone | Davy Crockett |
| Elizabeth Blackwell | Ferdinand Magellan | Francis Scott Key |
| Galileo | George Washington Carver | Harriet Tubman |
| Helen Keller | Henry Hudson | Jacques Cartier |
| Johnny Appleseed | Paul Bunyan | Robert Fulton |
| Rosa Parks | Sam Houston | |

**Library of Congress Cataloging-in-Publication Data**
Leavitt, Amie Jane.
  Christopher Columbus / by Amie Jane Leavitt.
    p. cm. — (A Robbie reader, What's so great about—?)
  Includes bibliographical references and index.
  ISBN 978-1-58415-578-2 (library bound)
  1. Columbus, Christopher—Juvenile literature. 2. Explorers—America—
Biography—Juvenile literature. 3. Explorers—Spain—Biography—Juvenile literature.
4. America—Discovery and exploration—Spanish—Juvenile literature.  I. Title.
E111.L435 2008
970.01'5092—dc22
[B]
                                                                                    2007000811

**ABOUT THE AUTHOR:** Amie Jane Leavitt is the author of numerous articles, puzzles, workbooks, and tests for kids and teens. She is a former teacher who has taught all subjects and grade levels. Ms. Leavitt loves to travel, play tennis, and learn new things every day. She, too, believes in following your dreams.

**PHOTO CREDITS:** Cover, pp. 1, 3, 4, 7, 16, 19, 26—Library of Congress; p. 6—Alejo Fernández/photo by Manuel Rosa; p. 8—Gaetano Guadagnini; p. 12—Jonathan Scott; p. 15—North Wind Picture Archives; p. 18—John Hagan; p. 24—Michael Zalewski; p. 27—Barbara Marvis.

**PUBLISHER'S NOTE:** The following story has been thoroughly researched and to the best of our knowledge represents a true story. While every possible effort has been made to ensure accuracy, the publisher will not assume liability for damages caused by inaccuracies in the data, and makes no warranty on the accuracy of the information contained herein.

PPC

# TABLE OF CONTENTS

Words in **bold** type can be found in the glossary.

King Ferdinand and Queen Isabella of Spain paid for Columbus's voyages. After his first voyage, Columbus returned to Spain. He brought the king and queen gifts of fruits and plants from the islands. He also brought back some of the Taino people.

# A Hero Returns

A grand parade marched through the narrow streets of Barcelona (bar-suh-LOH-nuh). People came out of their houses and cheered. Everyone wanted to see the hero of Spain. His name was Christopher Columbus. He had just found a new way to the Indies, a land rich in spices.

King Ferdinand and Queen Isabella (is-uh-BEL-uh) thought Columbus was important too. They invited him to their palace. They asked him to eat dinner at their table.

Columbus brought presents for the king and queen. He gave them fruit and flowers. He

Christopher Columbus opened the **New World** for exploration. His voyages had a lasting effect, both positive and negative, on the entire world.

gave them a type of colorful bird that they had never seen before. He even brought back **natives** (NAY-tivs) wearing jewelry made of gold.

The king and queen were excited. They liked listening to his stories about the beautiful islands. They asked him to go back and set up a

**colony** (KAH-luh-nee) there. They also wanted him to find gold and riches for Spain.

Before Columbus left, the king and queen gave him a new title. From that day on, he would be called Admiral of the Ocean Sea. They thought he was the greatest sea captain alive.

King Ferdinand and Queen Isabella were so pleased with Columbus's success on his first voyage that they gave him more money and ships to return to the "Indies."

Christopher Columbus left home at an early age to become a sailor on a merchant ship. Yet he never forgot his family. He always sent money home to help support his aged father, who had little money to take care of his needs.

# Dreaming of the Sea

Christopher Columbus was born in 1451. He was the first child of Susanna and Domenico (doh-MEN-ih-koh) Colombo. His parents had three more boys and one girl. Christopher had hair as red as fire and eyes as blue as the sea. His family was Catholic. Christopher had a strong faith in God his whole life.

Domenico was a weaver. He made fancy clothing for rich people. As a young boy, Christopher helped his father weave cloth. Yet Christopher didn't want to do this forever. He dreamed of going to sea.

Christopher was lucky to be born in Genoa ( JEH-noh-uh), Italy. This town is near the Mediterranean (meh-dih-tur-AY-nee-un) Sea. Many people in Genoa made their living on the sea. They fished or traveled on ships to sell goods to other cities. Christopher wanted to explore the big blue sea, too.

At age fourteen, Christopher did just that. He was hired to help on a **merchant** ship. He sailed south to Africa and north to Iceland. He loved his job.

At age twenty-five, he was shipwrecked. Christopher floated to shore on a piece of wood. He landed in a country called Portugal (PORT-choo-gul).

Christopher stayed there for many years. One of his brothers, Bartholomew (bar-THAH-lem-yoo), lived there, too. The two brothers sold maps and tools for sailors.

Christopher spent his free time reading books. He wanted to learn more about sailing and **geography** (jee-AH-gruh-fee). He had gone to school for a few years, but then he

The town of Genoa, Italy, built this monument for Christopher Columbus. (In Italian, his name is spelled Cristofòro Colombo.) He was born in Genoa in 1451.

taught himself as much as he could from books. Christopher still dreamed of the places he wanted to visit on the blue sea.

Christopher married Doña Felipa (DOH-nyah feh-LEE-puh) Moniz in 1479. They had a son named Diego (dee-AY-goh). Doña Felipa died when Diego was five years old. Soon, father and son moved to Spain. There, Christopher met Beatriz (BEE-uh-triz). They had a son named Ferdinand in 1488.

**11**

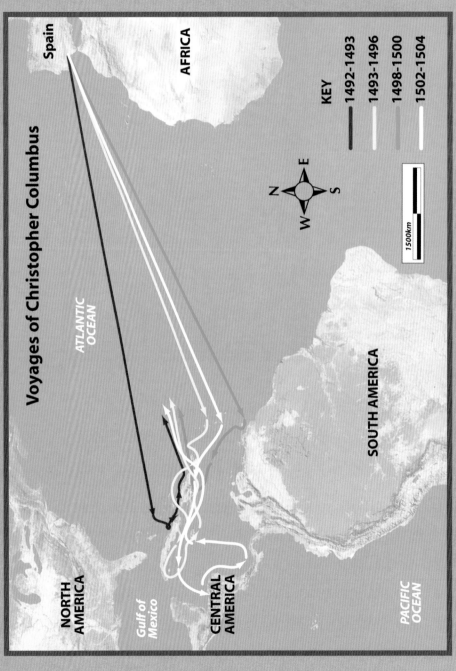

## Voyages of Christopher Columbus

**Spain**

**AFRICA**

ATLANTIC OCEAN

NORTH AMERICA

Gulf of Mexico

CENTRAL AMERICA

SOUTH AMERICA

PACIFIC OCEAN

**KEY**

— 1492-1493
— 1493-1496
— 1498-1500
— 1502-1504

N
W    E
S

1500km

Christopher Columbus went on a total of four voyages to what he called the Indies. Some people believe he explored areas of North America. However, during his four voyages, Columbus only landed on the islands of the Caribbean and in areas of Central and South America.

# Sailing West to the Indies

Columbus knew many sailors who wanted to find a way to the Indies. This area of the world is now called Asia. Back then, many people wanted spices and silk from the Indies, but the road between Europe and Asia was long and dangerous. Sailors wanted to find a safer and faster way by going east on the sea.

Not everyone thought sailing east was best. Columbus was one of those. He thought it would be better to sail west on the Ocean Sea. Today, this sea is called the Atlantic Ocean. In Columbus's time, this ocean was big and scary. Some people thought monsters lived in it. No one had ever tried to sail very far west on it. They were afraid they would be lost forever if they did.

Many people laughed at Columbus. They thought his ideas were crazy. But Columbus didn't care what people thought. He was not afraid of the Ocean Sea. He knew there was land out there somewhere.

He tried to get money for his trip. When King John II of Portugal said no, Columbus asked King Ferdinand and Queen Isabella for help.

At first the Spanish king and queen didn't think it was a good idea either. Then Queen Isabella thought more about it. She thought he was a smart person, and she felt she could trust him. She decided to give Columbus a chance.

Christopher Columbus began his journey on September 8, 1492. He had three ships: the *Niña* (NEE-nyuh), the *Pinta* (PEEN-tuh), and the *Santa María*. The three ships carried a total of ninety men and were filled with food, supplies,

Columbus presents his ideas to Queen Isabella and King Ferdinand of Spain. He believed that there was a westward route to Asia. The king and queen thought his idea was worth a try and agreed to pay for the voyage.

and water. The men had enough to last them one year. Columbus didn't think it would take that long to reach the Indies, but the men brought enough just in case it did.

Columbus landed in the New World on October 12, 1492. To the day
he died, he still believed he had found islands in the Indies.

# Land, Land!

Every night, Columbus said a prayer and wrote in his **journal**. He described the journey and wrote about what he and his men saw. One night, a bright streak of light splashed across the sky. It was a **meteor** (MEE-tee-or), but the crew didn't know this. They thought it was a sign to go back to Spain. Another time, they saw a ship's **mast** floating in the water. The men were afraid that their ship would sink too.

It wasn't too long before they came to the Sargasso (sar-GAA-soh) Sea. In this place in the Atlantic Ocean, seaweed floats on the surface for miles. Once they saw this, the sailors were very afraid. What if their ship got stuck in these slimy green sea plants?

On September 15, Columbus wrote: "The sea is less salty . . . and the breezes are more gentle. Everyone is cheerful, and the *Pinta,* the fastest sailing vessel, went ahead as fast as it could in order to sight land. . . . I trust Almighty God, in whose hands are all victories, will soon deliver us to land."

The men wanted to turn back many times. Columbus never did. He just kept saying, *"Adelante"* (aa-dih-LON-tay). In Spanish, this means "move forward."

On October 12, the cry of "Land, Land!" was heard. A few hours later, some of the men rowed ashore. They had finally made it to the Indies—or so they thought.

Columbus and his men weren't in the Indies at all. They had landed on an island in

Ships are too large to sail close to shore, so Columbus and his men had to anchor their three ships farther out in the water. They rowed to shore in smaller boats.

the Caribbean (kuh-RIH-bee-un), a sea between modern-day Florida and Mexico. Columbus had just found a place that was new to people in Europe (YUR-up).

Columbus thought the green, warm island was beautiful. He saw many new things. For one, the people who lived there had brown skin and didn't wear any clothing. This surprised Columbus and his men. The natives must have thought that Columbus and his men were unusual too. Why were they wearing so many clothes? And why was their skin so pale?

Columbus wrote in his journal about the native peoples on the islands: "They are of the opinion that I come from the sky." The natives gave Columbus and his men gifts, food, and water.

Columbus and his men could not understand the natives' language. If they could, they would have found out that these people were members of the Taino (TY-noh) tribe. Columbus thought he was in the Indies, so he called them Indians instead.

Columbus wanted to show that he came in peace. He gave the Taino glass beads as presents. The Taino gave him cotton thread, darts, and brightly colored birds called parrots.

Columbus left this island and the friendly Taino. The three ships sailed to many other islands in the area. Columbus noticed that some of the natives wore small gold jewelry. He had promised to find riches for the king and queen, so he convinced the natives to tell him where to find gold. They told him it was in Cuba. "I am now certain that Cuba is the Indian name for Japan," he wrote in his journal. Columbus still thought he was in Asia.

Columbus arrived on the island of Cuba on October 28. He rowed ashore with some of his men. They saw several houses on the shore. Columbus and his men went inside. The people weren't there, but their things were. They saw "nets made of palm threads, cords, fishhooks made of horn, harpoons made from bone, and other fishing materials," Columbus wrote. But Columbus respected these people's things. He "ordered that not one thing be touched." According to Columbus, his men obeyed.

Columbus went to many islands on this first voyage. He didn't find any gold, but he did find interesting plants and flowers. He took some of these on his ships. He also took some of the native people with him. He wanted to show them to the king and queen of Spain.

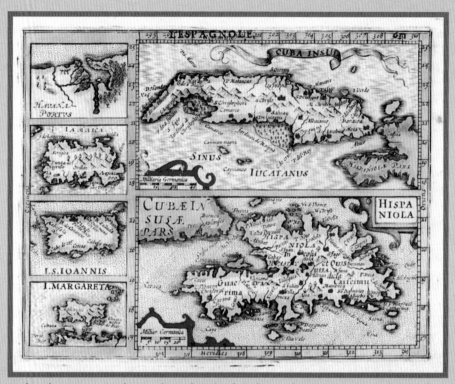

Columbus wrote about the island of Cuba in his journal on the evening of October 28, 1492: "I have never seen anything so beautiful. The country around the river is full of trees, beautiful and green and different from ours, each with flowers and its own kind of fruit. There are many birds of all sizes that sing very sweetly, and there are many palms different from those in Guinea or Spain."

# A New World

Columbus sailed to the New World three more times. On every voyage, he found places that no other European had ever seen. He landed in many places in Central America. He even landed in South America.

The New World had many treasures. Different kinds of plants grew there—including plants that people could use for food, tools, or trade. There were potatoes, pineapples, corn, tomatoes, chocolate, cotton, and tobacco (tuh-BAA-koh). The natives made long boats out of logs called canoes. They slept in swinging beds of rope called hammocks. All of these products were new to Columubus, and they became important to people in Europe, too.

The Taino had an advanced way of life. They grew their own crops, like yucca, sweet potatoes, corn, squash, peppers, and peanuts. They also fished and hunted for their meat. The women made pottery. Pieces of their pots and dishes continue to be found on the islands.

A re-created Taino village in Cuba. There were once millions of Taino in the Caribbean. Within 45 years of Columbus's arrival, they were all gone.

The Taino called their island Guanahani. Columbus gave it the Spanish name San Salvador. It was "in honor of our Lord and Savior who has granted me this miracle," he wrote in a letter on his return trip to Spain.

Columbus's voyages were a great achievement for the Europeans, but they had a terrible impact on the native peoples of the New World. Many natives died after the Europeans came. Some died of disease that Europeans brought with them. Others died in battles over land rights.

The Europeans wanted to find gold. They forced many of the natives to work in mines. These slaves would work long hours with little food and water. If they didn't find any gold, they might be killed.

Some sources say that Columbus was one of the people who made slaves of the Native Americans. Others claim that other European leaders were responsible for the poor treatment of the Native Americans. Regardless, after Columbus and his men landed in the New World in 1492, Native American culture in the Caribbean was lost.

Columbus finished his last voyage in 1504 and sailed back to Spain for the last time. He

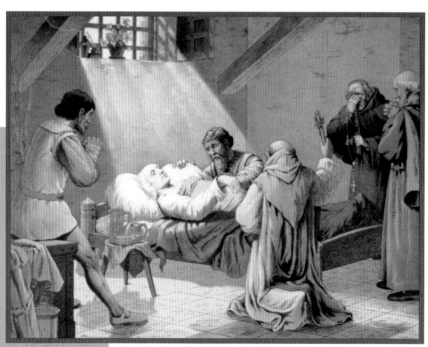

The Columbus family was at Christopher's side when he died in 1506.

The body of Christopher Columbus was first buried in this tomb in Seville, Spain. Later, it was supposed to be dug up and sent to the New World. No one knows if it was or not. Christopher Columbus's burial site remains a mystery.

had explored many islands on his four trips. He felt old and tired. Soon, he became very ill. Two years later, on May 20, 1506, he died. His family was by his side.

Columbus was a great explorer. He dared to go places that no European had ever gone before. He believed that the islands he found were in the Indies. What he really found was part of what would someday be called America.

# CHRONOLOGY

**1451** Christopher Columbus is born in Genoa, Italy.

**1468** He sets sail at the age of 14 on a merchant ship.

**1476** He is shipwrecked and swims ashore to the coast of Portugal. He works in Portugal selling maps with his brother Bartholomew.

**1479** Christopher marries Doña Felipa Moniz.

**1480** Their son, Diego, is born.

**1484** Columbus asks King John II of Portugal to support his exploration but is denied.

**1484** Doña Felipa dies.

**1485** Columbus moves to Spain with Diego.

**1488** Christopher's second son, Ferdinand, is born to Beatriz Enríquez de Harana.

**1492** Christopher convinces King Ferdinand and Queen Isabella of Spain to pay for his trip to the Indies. He leaves Spain on August 2 and lands in the New World on October 12.

**1493** He leaves on his second voyage to the New World and returns in 1496.

**1498** He begins his third voyage to the New World; he is gone until 1500.

**1502** His fourth voyage to the New World begins; it lasts until 1504.

**1506** He dies on May 20 in Valladolid, Spain.

# TIMELINE IN HISTORY

1400   The Renaissance begins in Europe.

1450   Johannes Gutenberg invents the printing press.

1452   Leonardo da Vinci is born.

1498   Vasco da Gama finds a water passage to the Indies by sailing around the southern tip of Africa.

1499   Amerigo Vespucci comes to the New World. North and South America are later named for him.

1500s  Europeans start the slave trade from Africa.

1519   Ferdinand Magellan sails around the world.

1534   England breaks away from the Catholic Church and starts the Church of England.

1584   Sir Walter Raleigh sets up the first English settlement in the New World at Roanoke Island, North Carolina.

1600s  Scientific revolution begins.

1609   Henry Hudson tries to find the Northwest Passage from Europe to Asia. He finds New York instead. The Hudson River, Hudson Bay, and Hudson Strait are named after him.

1776   American colonists write the Declaration of Independence.

1783   United States wins the Revolutionary War.

1787   United States Constitution is signed.

1804   Meriwether Lewis and William Clark set out to explore the new land bought by the United States—the Louisiana Purchase.

1812   United States and Great Britain fight the War of 1812.

1861   United States fights Civil War.

1886   Statue of Liberty is dedicated in New York harbor.

1912   Roald Amundsen leads the first expedition to the South Pole.

1914   World War I begins. It lasts until 1917.

1929   Stock market crashes. Great Depression begins.

1937   Columbus Day becomes a national holiday in the United States.

1939   World War II begins. It lasts until 1945.

1959   Yuri Gagarin, Russian cosmonaut, becomes first man in space.

1969   Neil Armstrong becomes the first man to walk on the moon.

1980   *Voyager I* is launched from Kennedy Space Center and travels to explore Saturn.

1996   Madeline Albright becomes first female Secretary of State.

2004   Mars Rover lands on Mars.

2007   NASA discovers new lakes on Saturn's largest moon, Titan.

# FIND OUT MORE

## Books

Macdonald, Fiona. *You Wouldn't Want to Sail with Christopher Columbus! Uncharted Waters You'd Rather Not Cross!* Danbury, Connecticut: Franklin Watts, 2004.

Sís, Peter. *Follow the Dream: The Story of Christopher Columbus.* New York: Knopf Books for Young Readers, 2003.

Wade, Mary Dodson. *Christopher Columbus: Famous Explorer.* (Graphic Biography). Mankato, Minnesota: Graphic Library, 2007.

## Works Consulted

Carroll, Frances Laverne. *Destination: Discovery! Activities and Resources for Studying Columbus and Other Explorers.* Chicago: American Library Association, 1994.

Columbus, Christopher. *The Journal of Christopher Columbus.* Translated by Cecil Jane. London: Anthony Blond, 1968.

Dotson, John, editor and translator. *Christopher Columbus and His Family: The Genoese and Ligurian Documents.* Turnhout, Belgium: Brepols, 1998.

Fernandez-Armesto, Felipe. *Columbus and the Conquest of the Impossible.* London: Phoenix Press, 1974.

McGovern, James R., editor. *The World of Christopher Columbus.* Macon, Georgia: Mercer University Press, 1992.

Morison, Samuel Eliot. *The Admiral of the Ocean Sea: A Life of Christopher Columbus.* Boston: Little, Brown and Company, 1942.

Sokolov, Raymond A. *Why We Eat What We Eat: How the Encounter Between the New World and the Old Changed the Way Everyone on the Planet Eats.* New York: Summit Books, 1991.

## On the Internet

BBC, Famous People: Christopher Columbus: http://www.bbc.co.uk/schools/famouspeople/standard/columbus/index.shtml#focus

Glencoe, The Journey of Christopher Columbus: Beyond the Textbook http://www.glencoe.com/sec/socialstudies/btt/columbus/index.html

Library of Congress, Introduction to 1492: An Ongoing Voyage http://www.loc.gov/exhibits/1492/

# GLOSSARY

colony (KAH-luh-nee)—A settlement governed by a country far away.

geography (jee-AH-gruh-fee)—The study of the earth's surface.

journal (JER-nul)—A record of a person's experiences, or of daily events.

mast (MAAST)—A long pole on a ship that holds up the sails.

merchant (MER-chent)—A person who buys and sells goods.

meteor (MEE-tee-or)—A piece of matter traveling through space. It can form a bright streak across the sky when it enters the earth's atmosphere. It is sometimes called a shooting star.

native (NAY-tiv)—An original resident of a particular place.

New World—The land of the Americas, which in 1492 was new to Europeans.

# INDEX